HISTORY & GEOGRAPHY
OREGON, LAND OF FOREST

MW00686408

CONTENTS

Author: **Mary Vandermey**

Editor-In-Chief: Richard W. Wheeler, M.A.Ed.

Editor: Martha K. Baxter, M.A.

Consulting Editor: Howard Stitt, Th.M., Ed.D.

Revision Editor: Alan Christopherson, M.S.

Alpha Omega Publications®

804 N. 2nd Ave. E., Rock Rapids, IA 51246-1759

Learn with our friends:

When you see me, I will help your teacher explain the exciting things you are expected to do.

When you do actions with me, you will learn how to write, draw, match words, read, and much more.

You and I will learn about matching words, listening, drawing, and other fun things in your lessons.

OREGON, LAND OF FORESTS

Imagine you have fifty pieces of wood cut into the shapes of all the fifty states of the United States. You have all of them in place except one piece. It is almost square with a dip in the center at the top. Fit it into the place you have left so that the west side touches the Pacific Ocean. The north side touches the state of Washington. The south is shared by California and Nevada. On the east you will see the state of Idaho. The state you have fitted into your finished puzzle is Oregon.

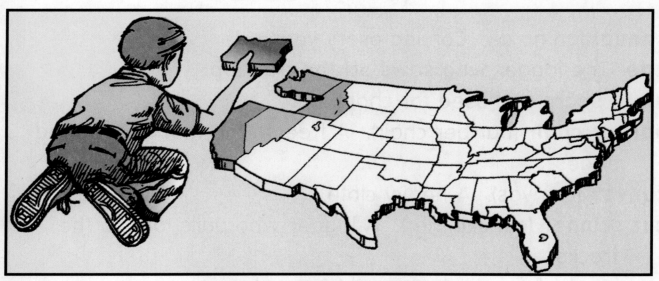

Oregon Fits into Place

My name is

Objectives

Read these objectives They tell you what you will be able to do when you have finished this LIFEPAC®.

1. You will be able to tell about Oregon and its forests.
2. You will be able to tell about the jobs of different lumbermen.
3. You will be able to tell how a new forest is started.
4. You will be able to tell how men fight forest fires.

NEW WORDS

annual (an nu al). Coming every year.

ape The logger who saws off the tree top.

ax A sharp tool used for chopping.

barber chair (bar ber chair). A tree stump that has ragged edges.

canvas (can vas). A heavy cloth.

cat skinner (cat skin ner). A logger who pulls logs to the trucks.

chemical (chem i cal). Something used to stop fires.

chopper (chop per). A logger who chops a notch in a tree.

community (com mu ni ty). All the people living in the same place.

conifer (con i fer). A tree that has cones.

dynamite (dy na mite). Something used to blow things into small pieces.

fire spotter (fire spot ter). The man who lives in the forest and watches for fires.

gopherman (go pher man). A logger who removes the tree trunks.

grader (grad er). A logger who sorts the lumber into poor, better, or best qualities.

hatchet (hatch et). A small ax.

high climber (high climb er). The logger who cuts off the short branches of the tall trees.

jack ladder (jack lad der). The ramp used to move logs into the sawmill from the water.

jack monkey (jack mon key). The logger who works at moving the logs up the jack ladder.

jagged (jag ged). With sharp points sticking out.

kiln Oven for drying.

lava (la va). The hot rock flowing from a volcano.

logging show (log ging show). The name of the logging work from start to finish.

lumber (lum ber). Timber that has been cut into boards.

lumberjack (lum ber jack). A man who works in the forest.

metal (met al). A very hard material.

nursery (nurs er y). A place where plants are grown.

peeler picker (peel er pick er). The logger who chooses the cut trees that will be sent to the sawmill.

product (prod uct). Anything that is made.

rigger slinger (rig ger sling er). The logger who fastens the logs so the lifting machine can move them.

river rat (riv er rat). The logger who works with the logs on the river.

selfish (sel fish). Caring too much for yourself and caring too little for others.

smoke jumper (smoke jum per). The man who jumps from a plane to fight fires in the forest.

spike A sharp pointed piece.

stomach robber (stom ach rob ber). The cook in the lumber camps.

stump The lower part of the tree left after the top is cut off.

timber (tim ber). Trees or forests that give wood for building.

tractor (trac tor). A powerful engine with wheels used to pull things.

trail blazer (trail blaz er). The logger who cuts roads into the forest where the cutting is to be done.

tree spotter (tree spot ter). The logger who picks out the trees to be cut.

volcano (vol ca no). A mountain with an opening from which steam and lava come out.

watch tower (watch tow er). The tall building where the men watch for forest fires.

waterproof (wat er proof). Able to keep water from coming in.

worm An animal that has no legs.

These words will appear in **boldface** (darker print) the first time they are used.

I. LOOKING AT OREGON

You will read about the state of Oregon in this LIFEPAC. In this section you will find how Oregon is special. You will learn about the forests in Oregon. In the forests are some enemies of the many trees. You will learn about these enemies also.

VOCABULARY

community	(com mu ni ty)	All the people living in the same place.
conifer	(con i fer)	A tree that has cones.
lava	(la va)	The hot rock flowing from a volcano.
lumber	(lum ber)	Timber that has been cut into boards.
product	(prod uct)	Anything that is made.
selfish	(sel fish)	Caring too much for yourself and caring too little for others.
timber	(tim ber)	Trees or forests that give wood for building.

volcano   (vol ca no)   A mountain with an opening from which steam and lava come out.

worm   An animal that has no legs.

SPECIAL WORDS

California	Oregon	Redwood
Christian	Oregon Trail	Spruce
Douglas Fir	Pacific Ocean	United States
Idaho	Ponderosa	Washington
Nevada		

Ask your teacher to say these words with you. Teacher check _____

Initial   Date

LAND OF THE FOREST

What would you see if you flew over Oregon in a plane? You would see great mountains. Many of them are snow-capped.

Much of the land is covered with forests. Other land is covered with **lava**. Where you see lava you know that **volcanoes** have spilled out hot rock at one time. The seacoast is rocky and beautiful. The rivers that flow through the state look like blue ribbons across the land.

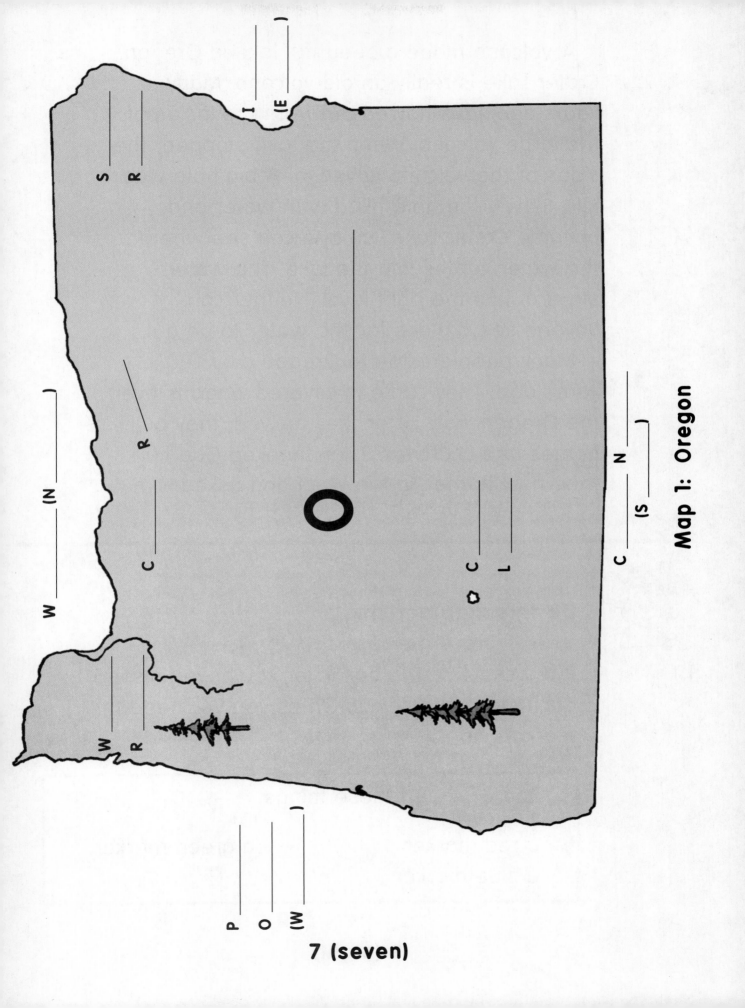

Map 1: Oregon

7 (seven)

A volcano made a beautiful lake in Oregon. Crater Lake is really an old volcano. Many years ago, lava flowed out from the inside of the large volcano. When the lava stopped, the sides of the volcano caved in. A big hole was left. Slowly the hole filled with water and became Crater Lake. No one can see where the water comes into the lake. The water stays at just the right level. Neither can anyone see a place for the water to go out.

Many people came to Oregon over 100 years ago. They came in covered wagons over the Oregon Trail. After they arrived, they built homes and churches. They thanked God for their new homes in the West and asked Him to help them.

Do this map activity.

1.1 Put a check in the box after you have finished each step. In later activities you will need the markers, too.

> You will need these things:
>
> a red marker   a green marker
> a blue marker

Use the map of Oregon (Map 1). The first letter of each word is printed on the map.

☐　　Print the word Oregon in large letters in red.

☐　　Print north, south, east and west in green.

☐　　Print the states that border Oregon in red.

☐　　Trace the rivers and print their names in blue.

☐　　Mark the Columbia River, the Snake River, and the Willamette River.

☐　　Mark the Pacific Ocean in blue.

Teacher check _____

　　　　　　　　　　　Initial　　　　　　　　　　Date

Today the people in Oregon live on farms and in towns. They have churches and schools. Many people working together make up the **communities**. Many people work in the large forests. Lumbering is an important business in Oregon.

TREES OF THE FOREST

You have already learned that much of the land in Oregon is covered with forests. Many trees fill these forests.

Do this map activity.

1.2　Put a check in the box when you have finished this step.

☐　Mark with a blue marker Crater Lake on your map.

9 (nine)

Write the answers to the questions in good sentences.

1.3   What formed Crater Lake? _____

_____

1.4   Where does Crater Lake get the water in it?

_____

_____

1.5   Where does the water go when it leaves Crater Lake? _____

_____

The most important tree of the Oregon forests is the Douglas fir. **Lumber** from the Douglas fir is sent to all parts of the country. The wood is used to make more **products** than any other tree in the world. The largest trees grow to be 300 feet tall. Some tree trunks are 10 feet wide. Many trees are said to be 700 years old.

Most **timber** trees are **conifers**. Trees which have seeds inside cones are called conifers. The Douglas fir tree is a conifer. Other trees found in the forests are spruce trees, ponderosa pines, and redwood trees. All of these are conifers.

Fill in the circle in front of the answer that goes in the blank.

1.6   Oregon has many _____.
        ○ grain fields   ○ fur lands   ○ forests

1.7   Volcanoes spill out hot _____.
        ○ soup   ○ lava   ○ dogs

1.8   The most important tree in the Oregon forest is the _____.
        ○ Douglas fir   ○ Cat fur   ○ Dog fur

1.9   The largest trees are _____ tall.
        ○ 30 feet   ○ 3,000 feet   ○ 300 feet

1.10   A 10-foot wide tree trunk is _____.
        ○ very weak   ○ very wide   ○ very narrow

1.11   Some trees are said to be _____ years old.
        ○ 700   ○ 7,000   ○ 70

1.12   A tree that has cones is called a _____.
        ○ conefur   ○ conifer   ○ content

1.13   Spruce, ponderosa, and redwood are _____ trees.
        ○ cone-bearing   ○ fruit   ○ small

1.14   People came to Oregon on the _____.
        ○ Washington Trail   ○ Oregon Trail   ○ Pacific Trail

Do these word activities.

1.15   Write a word in the blank. Use a word with a long
        /ē/ sound from the list.

        fear   cheer   hear   tear   deer   appear

        The high climber must not _____ being up high.

        A _____ may be seen among the trees.

        Did you _____ the men call, "Timber!"

        First to _____ is the trail blazer.

        The men _____ when the tree falls.

1.16   Unsafe has two syllables. The prefix un- is one
        syllable. The root word safe is one syllable.

        Divide the words into syllables. Write the syllables
        below the words. The first word is done for you.

                    be\low   unkind
        __be__   __low__   _____   _____

                    inside   disclose
        _____   _____   _____   _____

                    reread   untrue
        _____   _____   _____   _____

12 (twelve)

ENEMIES OF THE FOREST

Trees are large and strong, but they have enemies, too. One enemy is the insect. Insects eat into the trunks and roots of trees. Leaf-eating **worms** and insects can cause much harm to forests. A tree will die if the leaves are eaten. Birds help to protect the forests by eating many insects and worms.

Another enemy is the wolf tree. If trees grow too close together, they cannot get enough sunlight. They cannot find enough water. Sometimes a tree grows too wide. This kind of tree is called a wolf tree. The other trees do not have enough space. A wolf tree could be called a **selfish** tree, because it wants all the water and sun for itself. Lumbermen try to find these trees and cut them down before they spoil the neighboring trees.

One of the greatest enemies of the forest is fire when it burns out of control. Each year many trees are lost to fire. Lightning causes many fires. Other fires are started by careless people in the forests. Everyone must be very careful with campfires when camping in a forest.

ENEMIES OF THE FOREST

Insects

Wolf Tree

Fire

Do this map activity.

1.17   Check the box after you have finished this step.
    ☐ Circle the trees on Map 1. This symbol
      means forests are there.

Draw a line to match the words.

1.18	insects	burns trees
1.19	Douglas fir	have cones
1.20	wolf tree	carried people
1.21	conifers	protect trees
1.22	covered wagon	eat leaves
1.23	fire	an important business
1.24	birds	is selfish
1.25	lumbering	makes good lumber

Complete this reading activity.

1.26   Go to a special book to find out more about Oregon. Check the box after you have finished each step.

☐   Draw the Oregon state flag on another piece of paper.

☐   Draw the Oregon state bird.

☐   Draw the Oregon state tree.

Teacher check _____

Initial   Date

For this Self Test, study what you have read and done. The Self Test will check what you remember.

SELF TEST 1

Print yes **or** no **in front of each sentence.**

1.01   _____   A wolf tree helps other trees of the forest.

1.02   _____   Volcanoes once spilled lava in Oregon.

1.03   _____   The Oregon Trail was made by automobiles.

1.04   _____   Conifer means that the tree has apples on it.

1.05   _____   Washington borders Oregon on the north.

1.06   _____   Douglas fir trees make good lumber.

1.07   _____   Birds are enemies of the forest.

1.08   _____   Some of the tree trunks are very wide.

1.09   _____   The Pacific Ocean borders Oregon on the west.

1.010   _____   Early settlers built churches.

Draw a line to match the words.

1.011   Oregon   cones

1.012   volcanoes   selfish

1.013   tree trunk   west

1.014   conifer   eat leaves

1.015   insects   state

1.016   wolf tree   lava

1.017   Pacific Ocean   10-feet wide

Fill in the circle in front of the right answer.

1.018   Some Douglas fir trees may be _____ years old.
         ○   10   ○   300   ○   700

1.019   Enemies of the forest are _____.
         ○   birds and   ○   insects and   ○   rain and
             cats   fire   snow

1.020   On the east side of Oregon is _____.
         ○   Kansas   ○   Maine   ○   Idaho

Teacher check _____

                    Initial   Date

EACH ANSWER, 1 POINT

16
20

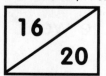

My Score

16 (sixteen)

II. LUMBERING IN OREGON

Lumbering has changed since the work of cutting the trees began. In this section you will learn many new names that the lumbermen use for people and things in the lumbering business. Men who work in forests are sometimes called **lumberjacks**.

VOCABULARY

annual	(an nu al)	Coming every year.
ape		The logger who saws off the tree top.
ax		A sharp tool used for chopping.
barber chair	(bar ber chair)	A tree stump that has a ragged edge.
canvas	(can vas)	A heavy cloth.
cat skinner	(cat skin ner)	A logger who pulls logs to the trucks.
chopper	(chop per)	A logger who chops a notch in the tree.
dynamite	(dy na mite)	Something used to blow things into small pieces.

gopherman	(go pher man)	A logger who removes the tree stumps.
grader	(grad er)	A logger who sorts the lumber into poor, better or best qualities.
hatchet	(hatch et)	A small ax.
high climber	(high climb er)	The logger who cuts off the short branches of the tall trees.
jack ladder	(jack lad der)	The ramp used to move logs into the sawmill from the water.
jack monkey	(jack mon key)	The logger who works at moving the logs up the jack ladder.
jagged	(jag ged)	With sharp points sticking out.
kiln		Oven for drying.
logging show	(log ging show)	The name of the logging work from start to finish.
lumberjack	(lum ber jack)	A man who works in a forest.
metal	(met al)	A very hard material.
peeler picker	(peel er pick er)	The logger who chooses the cut trees that will be sent to the sawmill.

rigger slinger	(rig ger sling er)	The logger who fastens the logs so the lifting machine can move them.
river rat	(riv er rat)	The logger who works with the logs on the river.
spike		A sharp pointed piece.
stomach robber	(stom ach rob ber)	The cook in the lumber camps.
stump		The lower part of the tree left after the top is cut off.
tractor	(trac tor)	A powerful engine with wheels used to pull things.
trail blazer	(trail blaz er)	The logger who cuts roads into the forest where the cutting is to be done.
tree spotter	(tree spot ter)	The logger who picks out the trees to be cut.
waterproof	(wat er proof)	Able to keep water from coming in.

 Ask your teacher to say these words with you.
Teacher check _____
Initial   Date

WORK IN THE FOREST

When lumbering first began in Oregon, the men who owned the forest set up lumber camps. Men came to work. The **lumberjacks** lived in camps. The men had a camp cook. The men had a special name for their cook. They called him a **stomach robber** because often the food was not cooked right.

The lumbermen live in towns near the forests now. Their children go to school. The families go to church on Sunday.

Camp Cook

A **logging show** is the name of the work that must be done from start to finish. At the start of the logging show, the owner of the lumber business tells the **trail blazers** which trees he wants cut. The trail blazers cut roads into the forests where the cutting is to be done.

Before any tree is cut, a **tree spotter** goes through the forest and decides which trees are best to cut. He looks for

HISTORY & GEOGRAPHY

GEOGRAPHY

3 0 4

LIFEPAC TEST

24 / 30

Name _____

Date _____

Score _____

HISTORY & GEOGRAPHY 304: LIFEPAC TEST

EACH ANSWER, 1 POINT

Write yes **or** no **in front of the sentences.**

1. _____ A wolf tree helps other trees in the forest.
2. _____ Good lumbermen replace the trees they have cut.
3. _____ Douglas firs make good lumber.
4. _____ Insects hurt trees.
5. _____ People came to Oregon on the Kansas Trail.
6. _____ The most important business in Oregon is lumbering.
7. _____ Some tree trunks are very wide.
8. _____ A jagged cut tree is a rocking chair.
9. _____ Planes are used to fight fires.
10. _____ Lumbermen have an easy job.

Fill in the circle in front of the right answers.

11. The whole job of cutting trees to take them to the sawmill is called _____.
    ○ car show   ○ wood show   ○ logging show

12. A kiln is used for _____ the lumber.
    ○ wetting   ○ drying   ○ storing

13. A river rat's job is to _____.
    ○ break up a log jam   ○ watch for boats   ○ swim fast

1 (one)

14. When a tree is about to fall the men yell, "_____!"
   ○ Logs   ○ Forest   ○ Timber
15. The age of a tree can be told by the _____.
   ○ rings   ○ shoes   ○ hats

Choose each answer from the list. Write it on the line.

dynamite   ape
chemicals   smoke jumper
volcano   weather
nursery   conifer
truck   tree spotter

16.   A lumberman buys new trees at a _____.
17.   Planes are used to put _____ and water on fires.
18.   Forest fires are spread by winds and dry _____.
19.   The man who jumps from a plane to help put out fires
      is a _____.
20.   Crater Lake was caused by a _____.
21.   The man who says which trees are to be cut is a
      _____.
22.   The man who cuts off the top of the tree is called the
      _____.
23.   Usually, logs are taken from the forests by _____.
24.   To break up a log jam, _____ is used.
25.   A tree that has cones is called a _____.

Write five things made of wood.

26. _____

27. _____

28. _____

29. _____

30. _____

NOTES

straight trees that are healthy. If insects have eaten into a tree, the lumber from that tree would be full of holes. The trees must have the right thickness, too. If the trees are not thick enough, they will not make enough lumber.

When the spotter chooses a tree to be cut, he paints a capital C on the tree. Also, he marks on the tree where the tree is to be cut.

The **high climber** is one of the bravest men in the forest. He climbs up the high Douglas fir trees. He wears a safety belt and **spiked** shoes. As he climbs, he cuts off short tree branches with his **hatchet.** When he has cut all the little branches, he climbs down.

An Ape

The next man is called an **ape**, because he climbs even higher than the high climber. He is fastened safely to wires from a machine. When he reaches the spot where the top of the tree should be cut off, he saws the tree top off. Then he comes down the tree.

Write a sentence to tell what each of these logging words mean.

2.1   logging show _____

_____

2.2   trail blazer _____

_____

2.3   tree spotter _____

_____

2.4   high climber _____

_____

2.5   ape _____

_____

2.6   stomach robber _____

_____

After the climbers and the apes have done their work, the **choppers** take over. These men wear special clothes called tin pants and coats. The clothes are not really tin. They are made of heavy **waterproof canvas**. The clothes protect the choppers from scratches and rain. Also, the chopper wears a hard hat, which is a **metal** hat that protects his head.

The chopper sees the big C on the tree. He chops a notch with an **ax**. The notch helps the tree to fall where the men want it to fall.

Next, the men with electric saws cut the tree. As the tree begins to fall, the men call out through the forest, "Timber!" Everyone knows to watch out for the falling tree when they hear "Timber!"

The tree is cut.

A Barber Chair

Usually a tree is cut straight across. Sometimes a tree will snap off before the saws cut straight through. **Jagged** edges are left on the **stump**. The stump is called a **barber chair**.

Tree Rings

After a tree is cut, the rings on the inside of the trunk can be seen. These rings are called **annual** rings. One ring is added each year as the tree grows older. The annual rings never change after they are formed. The thick rings show a year of a lot of rain. The thin rings show a year of little rain.

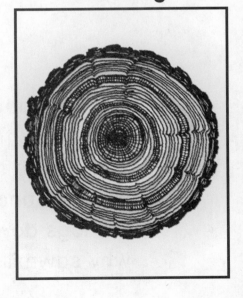

23 (twenty-three)

Next a **peeler picker** looks at the tree that has been cut down. He looks at it many times. He decides if the tree trunk should be cut into lumber at the sawmill. The best trees go to the sawmill to be made into lumber. The other trees go to be used to make other wooden products.

A **rigger slinger** starts to work. He fastens the log so that a lifting machine can move it.

The **cat skinner** pulls the logs across the forest with a big **tractor** called a cat. Many cat skinners are pulling logs to where the trucks are. The logging trucks take the logs out of the forest. Strong chains keep the logs on the trucks.

**The cat
pulls the logs.**

If the cat skinner takes the logs to the sawmill by truck, then he has a long drive. Sometimes the cat skinner takes the logs to the river and lets the power of the river take the logs downstream to the sawmill. That is why sawmills are beside the rivers. The logs are dumped into the water. Sometimes the logs float separately. Other times they are tied together and pulled to the mill by boat.

The river takes the logs to the sawmill.

Sometimes the floating logs pile up at a bend in the river. The **river rats** must free the log jam. They jump from log to log poking the logs with a long stick. They separate the logs and start the logs going down the river again. The river rats are brave. They are light and quick on their feet. One wrong step would put them in the river among the heavy logs. If they cannot break up the log jam with sticks, they must use **dynamite**. The dynamite blows the logs apart.

The logs are usually carried out of the forest on trucks. After the trucks leave the forest, the land must be made ready to plant again. **Gophermen** are in charge of removing the tree stumps. Sometimes dynamite is used to blow up the stumps and roots. The stumps are carried away by truck, too. Then trees are planted on the land again.

Do this reading activity

2.7   Safely has two syllables. The root word is safe. The suffix is -ly. The suffix -ly is one syllable. The root word safe is one syllable.

Divide the words into syllables. Write the syllables below the words. The first word is done for you.

slow\ly
slow ____   ____ ly ____   sixteen _____   _____

cheerful
_____ _____   cupful _____ _____

friendship
_____ _____   darkness _____ _____

Do this activity

2.8   Number these sentences in the order they happened in the story.

26 (twenty-six)

_____ Trucks carry logs out of the forest.

_____ A rigger slinger fastens logs to the lifting machine.

_____ The cat skinner pulls the logs across the forest with a cat.

_____ Men cut the trees.

_____ A high climber cuts off little tree branches.

_____ The ape cuts the tops off the trees to be cut down.

WORK AT THE SAWMILL

Near the mill is a pond where the logs are dumped by the trucks. Some logs may have come down the river to the pond. The jack monkey is working hard in the pond to keep the logs moving up the jack ladder to the mill. The logs go through the door of the mill.

Inside the mill, the logs are cut by saws into strips. The wooden strips are made smooth. Next, the lumber is put into a **kiln** to dry. Fresh lumber has much water in it. The kiln dries the wood until it is not too wet and not too dry.

The **grader** looks at the lumber and decides if the wood is a poor, good, better or best grade of lumber. The lumber that is not usable is ground up and used to make paper.

You use paper every day. Did you know that some of the paper you use was once part of a tree? Now you know how part of a tree became a piece of paper!

Do this activity.

2.9   Each word at the top of a list has the long /o͞o/ sound in it. The words have different letters for the long /o͞o/ sound. Circle the words in each list that have the long /o͞o/ sound.

food	**few**	**you**
moon	grow	cloud
foot	grew	soup
shook	know	through
stood	knew	mouse
good	flow	out
too	flew	sound

Answer the questions in good sentences.

2.10   What happens at the mill?_____

_____

_____

_____

2.11   What are four things made from wood?_____

_____

2.12   What is the job of a jack monkey? _____

_____

Match these words.

2.13   cat skinner   tin clothes
2.14   lumberjack   fastens logs to be lifted
2.15   river rat   dries lumber
2.16   chopper   picks best cut trees
2.17   dynamite   pulls logs with a tractor
2.18   peeler picker   frees log jams
2.19   rigger slinger   any lumberman
2.20   kiln   blows up log jams

Teacher check _____

                          Initial   Date

Study what you have read and done for this Self Test. This Self Test will check what you remember of this part and other parts you have read.

SELF TEST 2

Write the words that go in the blanks. Choose an answer from the list.

sawmill	cut	selfish	barber chair
falling	lumber	log jam	rings
volcanoes	branches		

2.01   If you hear the word, "Timber!" it means a tree is

_____ .

2.02   Tree spotters say which trees are to be _____ .

2.03   A pile-up of logs in a river is called a _____ .

2.04   Douglas fir trees make good _____ .

2.05   The tree's age is told by the _____ in a tree
log or stump.

2.06   In Oregon, _____ were once active.

2.07   A wolf tree is a tree that is _____ .

2.08   A jack monkey keeps the logs going into the _____ .

2.09   A tree stump that does not cut off smoothly is called a

_____ .

2.010   The high climber cuts little _____ off the tree
before the tree is cut down.

Write yes **or** no **on the lines in front of the sentences.**

2.011   _____   The Pacific Ocean is east of Oregon.

2.012   _____   People came to Oregon many years ago on
the Oregon Trail.

2.013 _____ Insects are good for trees.

2.014 _____ Many people must work hard to cut down trees.

2.015 _____ Men who work in lumbering use special names for workers.

2.016 _____ A logging show is a play.

2.017 _____ A stomach robber steals stomachs.

2.018 _____ Some paper is made from wood.

2.019 _____ Cars usually take the logs from the forest.

2.020 _____ A conifer has cones.

Draw lines to match the lumbermen with their jobs.

2.021   ape   cuts branches

2.022   high climber   says what trees are to be cut

2.023   tree spotter   gets logs into mill

2.024   trail blazer   cuts roads

2.025   jack monkey   cuts top of tree off

Teacher check _____

                Initial   Date

EACH ANSWER, 1 POINT

20	
	25

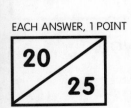

My Score

III. KEEPING OREGON'S FORESTS

You have read about the jobs of the different men who work in the forest. You learned what happens to the tree from cutting to the sawmill. Now you will read what happens to the land after the trees are cut. You will find how the forests are protected from fire.

VOCABULARY

chemical	(chem i cal)	Something used to stop fires.
fire spotter	(fire spot ter)	The man who lives in the forest and watches for fires.
nursery	(nurs er y)	A place where plants are grown.
smoke jumper	(smoke jum per)	The man who jumps from a plane to fight fires in the forest.
watch tower	(watch tow er)	The tall building where the men watch for forest fires.

 Ask your teacher to say these words with you.
Teacher check _____

Initial   Date

START OF A NEW FOREST

The lumbermen have taken many trees from the land. They have pulled the stumps that were left. The land is made ready for new trees, first. Then, most lumbermen buy their new supply of trees from people who grow little trees. Young trees are grown in **nurseries** until they are big enough to be in the forests.

Sometimes the lumbermen want to grow the new trees from seeds. A plane is used to fly over the land. The seeds are dropped from the plane. The seeds fall to the ground. Many seeds do not grow. Some are eaten by birds. Others fall on rocks. Many more seeds than the number of trees wanted are dropped from the plane.

After the trees start to grow, the new forests are thinned and cut. The lumbermen watch for the wolf trees and cut them. The forests are kept clean so that the little sticks and bushes will not help to feed a forest fire.

Do this reading activity.

3.1   Read the sentences. Add a suffix from the list to the underlined word to make a new word. Write the new word in the blank in the next sentence.

The <u>mountain</u> was very high. The _____ roads were covered with snow in the winter.

The <u>act</u> of the boy was very kind. The boy's _____ was kind.

I wonder if he can <u>collect</u> the money. The _____ will be used to help the sick boy.

The happy girl was filled with <u>joy</u>. She was _____ about the party.

Do these activities.

3.2   Write two sentences that tell how a lumberman replaces the trees he has cut for lumber.

        _____

        _____

3.3   How does a plane help to plant seeds? _____

        _____

        _____

FIRES IN THE FOREST

In a forest are men who live there and watch for fires. **Fire spotters** are stationed in **watch towers** in all the forests. The fire spotters look through powerful glasses for any smoke. In a storm, lightning can strike a tree and start a big fire.

When a fire spotter sees smoke coming up from the forest, he telephones or radios another watch tower. All the spotters in the forest want to know about any fire. The firemen are called, too. Sometimes the fires can be put out before they spread. The firemen use water and **chemicals** to put out the fires.

Planes fly low over the fire, and the water or chemicals fall on the fire. Often wind and dry weather help the fire to spread very fast. If a fire grows too large, thousands of trees can be lost in a short time.

Smoke jumpers are men who jump from planes near the fire to work at stopping the fire. They dig up the ground so that the fire cannot spread any farther. They start other fires that they can put out so that the big fire has nothing to burn when it reaches that spot. They throw dirt on the fire, too. Fires do not burn if they are covered.

All these men help to keep the forests green and beautiful in God's world. After a fire, the land is planted with trees again. The forests grow to cover the land. God gave us trees.

Answer the questions. Use good sentences in your answers.

3.4   What is the job of a smoke jumper? _____
_____

3.5   What do the fire spotters do when they see smoke in the forest? _____
_____

3.6   Where are little trees grown before they are sold?
_____
_____

3.7   What two things do firemen use to put out fires?
_____
_____

3.8   What two ways are planes used by men in the forests?_____

_____

3.9   What two things help to spread forest fires? _____

_____

_____

Teacher check _____
                        Initial   Date

Review
REVIEW
Review

Study what you have read and done for this last Self Test. This Self Test will check what you remember in your studies of all parts in this LIFEPAC. The last Self Test will tell you what parts of the LIFEPAC you need to study again.

SELF TEST 3

Write yes **or** no **on the line in front of the sentence.**

3.01 _____ Little trees are grown in a nursery.

3.02 _____ A wolf tree is a good tree.

3.03 _____ The first people to come to Oregon used the Oregon Trail.

3.04 _____ Lumbermen do not replant the forests they have cut.

3.05 _____ Douglas firs make good lumber.

3.06 _____ You can spread a log jam on your bread.

Write the correct word in the blank. Choose the words from the list.

cat skinner	water	ape
barber chair	jack monkeys	Oregon
gophermen	rings	smoke jumpers

3.07   Men who feed the logs into sawmills are called

_____.

3.08   Crater Lake is in _____.

3.09   Men who drive the big tractors are called _____

_____.

3.010   Men who jump into forests are called _____.

3.011   You can tell the age of a tree by the _____.

3.012   Firemen put _____ on the fire from the plane.

3.013   The tree stumps are removed by the_____.

3.014   The man who cuts the top from the tree is called

an _____.

3.015   A tree that is not cut straight is called a _____.

Draw lines to match the words.

3.016	state of forests	Idaho
3.017	west	California and Nevada
3.018	east	Pacific Ocean
3.019	north	Washington
3.020	south	Oregon

Teacher check _____
                    Initial   Date

EACH ANSWER, 1 POINT

16 / 20

My Score

Before taking the LIFEPAC Test, you should do these self checks.

1. _____ Did you do good work on your last Self Test?

2. _____ Did you study again those parts of the LIFEPAC you didn't remember?

   Check one: ☐ Yes (good)

               ☐ No (ask your teacher)

3. _____ Do you know all the new words in "Vocabulary"?

   Check one: ☐ Yes (good)

               ☐ No (ask your teacher)

NOTES

1492
Voyages of Columbus

Citizenshi

2001

World Trade Center Towers

1939

The Renaissa

World War II

The Middle Ages

1972

The Watergate Scandal

1861

American Civil War

Cattle in Texas

Fishing in Maine

Alpha Omega Publications®

804 N. 2nd Ave. E.
Rock Rapids, IA 51246-1759
800-622-3070
www.aop.com

HIS0304 – Jul '08 Printing

ISBN 978-0-86717-524-0

9 780867 175240

Nutrilicious

Food for Thought
and Whole Health

EDITH ROTHSCHILD